GIVE, EAT, AND LIVE

GIVE, EAT, AND LIVE

Poems of Avvaiyar

Translated from the Tamil
by
THOMAS HITOSHI PRUIKSMA

 RED HEN PRESS | *Pasadena, CA*

Give, Eat, Live: Poems of Avvaiyar

ISBN 978-1-63628-087-5 (tradepaper)

The National Endowment for the Arts, the Los Angeles County Arts Commission,
the Ahmanson Foundation, the Dwight Stuart Youth Fund, the Max Factor Family
Foundation, the Pasadena Tournament of Roses Foundation, the Pasadena Arts &
Culture Commission and the City of Pasadena Cultural Affairs Division, the City
of Los Angeles Department of Cultural Affairs, the Audrey & Sydney Irmas Char-
itable Foundation, the Kinder Morgan Foundation, the Meta & George Rosenberg
Foundation, the Allergan Foundation, the Riordan Foundation, Amazon Literary
Partnership, and the Mara W. Breech Foundation partially support Red Hen Press.

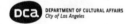

Second Edition
Published by Red Hen Press
www.redhen.org

For David Citino,

Sam Hamill,

and Dr. K. V. Ramakoti

TABLE OF CONTENTS

INTRODUCTION

The word *Auvai* means "mother," "older woman," or "female ascetic"; to it we add *ār*, a respectful suffix, to make "Avvaiyar" (Auvaiyār). The name has been given to women since the Sangam period, roughly 100 B.C.E. to 250 C.E. An Avvaiyar of that time was given the loving protection of Atiyamāṉ Netumāṉ Añci, one of the seven great patrons of the final Sangam, the literary fraternity or community. We know of this from the songs she sang. Her elegy upon his death is one of the undying treasures of Tamil literature, and many of her other poems are collected in the *Puṟanāṉūṟu*, among the oldest of the ancient anthologies.

The Avvaiyar of the translations that follow, who has given us books such as *Ātticcūṭi*, *Koṉṟaivēntan*, *Mūturai*, *Nalvaḻi*, and *Ñaṉakkuṟal*, is thought to have lived later, in the twelfth century. Her poems are cited in the work of commentators such as Pērāciriyar and Naccinārkkiṉiyar. She strove in these books to instill essential truths about life in the hearts of young children, composing *Ātticcūṭi* in short lines, *Koṉṟaivēntan* in longer lines, and *Mūturai* and *Nalvaḻi* in quatrains, sweet *venpā*. Everyone in Tamil Nadu who can read has read her poems. As the esteemed pundit N. M. Vēṅkaṭacāmi Nāṭṭaṉār has written, "It is the pride of Tamil Nadu to have been home to the woman that established this way of imparting practical wisdom to young people throughout the land."[1] Stories abound about her life, but since, as far as history is concerned, "tales give us false facts,"[2] it is better to set them aside. There is no doubt, however, that the fame of Avvaiyar, like that of the Avvaiyar before her, will live as long as the world lives.

Avvaiyar was clearly a devout woman. In *Mūturai* and *Nalvaḻi* she prays to Piḷḷaiyār (also known as Ganesh, son of Lord Shiva) and in *Nalvaḻi* she praises the five-letter mantra:

> For those who think upon *ci vā ya na ma*
> Not even one day of distress.
> This
> Is both way and wisdom ... (15)

Later she sings the greatness of marking the forehead with holy ash ("without it, a face is nothing"), and in *Nalvaḻi*'s final poem she celebrates the glorious hymnbooks to Shiva: *Tēvāram*, *Tiruvācakam*, *Tirukkōvai*, and

---

1.   Introduction to *Aththichoodi* (Tinnevelly: The South India Saiva Siddhanta Works Publishing Society, 1950): 4.

2.   Commentary by Aṭiyārkkunallār on *The Cilappatikāram of Iḷaṅkō Aṭikaḷ*, edited by U. Vē Cāmiṉātaiyar (Madras: Srī Tiyākarāca Vilāca Veliyītu, 1979 [1892]).

Tirumantiram. We can therefore say with certainty that she is Saivite, a follower of Lord Shiva. The final poem also shows us that she considered the *Tirukkuraḷ* and the *Upanishads*, two works of philosophy and ethics that have endured for millennia, to be of equally great importance.

In placing a prayer song at the beginning of her books, Avvaiyar follows a long tradition. Poets compose invocations of this kind in order to complete successfully the works that they begin. The invocations that open *Mūturai* and *Nalvaḻi*, however, are unusual and demonstrate the depth of her devotion.

In the opening prayer of *Mūturai*, Avvaiyar illustrates the earthly good of daily worship: Those who come daily before the coral-red body and trunk of Piḷḷaiyār, praying and placing fresh flowers at his feet, will receive powers of speech, a mind that thinks good thoughts, the wealth that comes from Lakshmi, and a body free of disease. God gives everything necessary to those who have a pure and unwavering faith. They are the ones who have his grace (*aruḷ*), and by this grace, can show others the right path. Avvaiyar is among them. All religions stress that true faith leads to blessings, and Avvaiyar tells us this too.

In the invocation to *Nalvaḻi*, Avvaiyar sings directly to Piḷḷaiyār: "I will make *koḻukkaṭṭai* from milk, clear honey, jaggery, and fragrant bengal gram, and give it all to you, Piḷḷaiyār with your radiant and pure elephant's face. Give me, in return, the three parts of Sangam Tamil." Anything made and given to god with devotion is a peerless gift; god receives it with joy and grants the blessings his devotees desire. Avvaiyar gives Piḷḷaiyār the *koḻukkaṭṭai* he loves; Piḷḷaiyār grants her the poetic riches of Sangam Tamil. And so the poems of this divinely blessed Avvaiyar are filled with the virtues of sweetness, simplicity, intensity, and unforgettability.

In these two invocations, then, Avvaiyar affirms two principles:

1) Devotees receive god's blessings in this life.

2) There is no shame in asking god for blessings.

In so doing, these two poems also show a way of approaching god.

In our tradition, those who believe in god also believe in fate or karma (*ūḻviṉai*). By karma a person is tempered over time, brought closer to god, and finally made one with god. God gives humans the freedom to choose their actions; they can do good or bad deeds as they desire. These deeds, in turn, good and bad alike, bind people to the wheel of rebirth. People return again and again and suffer endlessly on earth. Eventually, though, they want release from this anguish. They seek a way out. And they see that a holy teacher or guru is the one who shows people this way.

And what is the way? People must learn to live without attachment, like water on a lotus's leaves. In such a state, neither good nor bad deeds attach to a person's being. He has neither good nor bad karma; he does not see himself as distinct from other beings; he does not believe that his soul and the great soul—god—are separate. He reaches a state of true knowledge and wisdom.

Avvaiyar, as such a guru and saint, shows the way to achieve this wisdom, be released from the wheel of rebirth, and become one, at last, with god.

Mūturai and *Nalvaḻi*, then, are great works of literature in which such wisdom shines. Great poets—poets who write works that overcome time—attend closely to nature, to all that happens there, to the nature of all beings, joining what they see with the thoughts they wish to express and thus speaking in ways that delight and astonish us into praise. This is the way to make work that lasts, and Avvaiyar is a master of this way.

We have a saying in Tamil: "The work you point out with your feet I will do with my head." The person who says this shows his humility, gratitude, and respect, because he is willing to use the highest part of his body to do what has been asked by the lowest. In a similar fashion, a coconut palm takes plain water at its roots and returns it as sweet tender-coconut water from its crown. How high, how great, the heart-and-mind of a person who takes something ordinary and returns it extraordinary! One who has such a character is good; one who does not, is not. So sings Avvaiyar, impressing it on our hearts:

> When doing good to a man, do not ask
> If he'll do good.
> > Tall-standing coconut palms,
> Tireless and growing, take water at their roots
> And return it, sweet, from above. (1)

Avvaiyar gives us vivid images with which to grasp her ideas. Letters carved in stone do not fade; good done to a man of goodness is not forgotten. Letters written upon water vanish as they are made; good done to a man with no goodness in his heart is forgotten even as it's done. However long you boil milk, its flavor does not diminish; however long you heat a conch, its color does not change; until the moment it's cut down, a tree grants the people shade. No matter how much he suffers, a man of goodness remains good; he returns evil with good, and good alone. But a man without goodnessfalls prey to his anger; his friendships break apart as a stone pillar breaks. Like a tiger that eats even the one who helps him, he won't hesitate to do evil to his friends. But one cannot tell good people from bad by appearances alone. Looks and words can bewitch and deceive. Avvaiyar shows us that only through their actions and the nature revealed by those actions can we distinguish between kinds of people. So it is good to see a good person, to hear his or her good words, to seek out his or her friendship, just as it is bad to see an evil person, to hear his or her words, to seek out his or her friendship. The world is overrun with mirages that beguile and quicksands that confuse, but Avvaiyar travels with us, showing us which way is sound and which way is not. She is a poet and guide that shines.

We can place Avvaiyar in a tradition of wisdom-teaching literature that goes back to the Sangam period. Over two thousand years ago, the wise men and women of Tamil Nadu shared what they knew with the people. Many of their ideas correspond with contemporary thinking about the nature of people and the world. Look, for instance, at the following examples:

1) (A blessing on the land)
   Whether field or forest,
   Hillside or valley,
   You will be good
   Where the men are good.

   —Auvaiyār (Sangam period)

2) . . . . The good of wealth
   Is in giving. Enjoying it alone,
   A man commits errors of all kinds.

   —Nakkīranār (Sangam period)

3) Every place is home, every person kin.
   Good and evil do not come from others—
   Nor pain, nor release from pain. Death
   Is nothing new. We do not rejoice
   Saying life is sweet, nor say
   With disgust that it is bitter.
   As wood in a great river
   Goes forth on its way, carried by waters
   Cascading down rocks, by torrents
   From skies crisscrossed by lightning,
   So our dear lives
   Go where they must.
   Thus say the ones who have seen.
   So we, now, who see by their sight,

Are not amazed by the great—
Nor do we scorn the little.

                    —Kaṇiyaṉ Pūṅkuṉṟaṉār (Sangam period)

4)   . . . .
        If you cannot do good,
        At least shun evil.
        It will please all people
        And guide you, at last,
        To the right path.

                    —Nariverūuttalaiyār (Sangam period)

5)   Āy does not deal in good deeds, giving
        In this life for the sake of the next.
        He follows the way of wise men.
        From this, his generous hand.

                    —Ēṉiccēri Muṭamōciyār (Sangam period)

6)   Does Pēkaṉ–of great horses and wild elephants
        Give all that he gives thinking of the life to come?
        No. He thinks of those who have nothing. Thus
        His generous hand.

                    —Paraṇar (Sangam period)

7)   Wrong done to others before noon
        Comes back of its own by nightfall.

—The *Tirukkuṛaḷ* of Tiruvaḷḷuvar

Avvaiyar too has said truths in the way that the people of her time thought beautiful. Poets and sages sing their times, but the people praise and celebrate them in all times. Literature is always coming into being. It does not pass away. In the following poem from *Mūturai*, Avvaiyar describes a hard aspect of human life with the help of two scientific principles:

A cup that is plunged deep into the sea
Cannot yield four cups of water.
                           Even if
Both wealth and husband are yours, past deeds
Alone shape one's pleasure. (19)

We can see in the poem's first two lines the idea that pressure depends on depth and the idea that pressure does not affect the volume of liquids. How could Avvaiyar have known this? She might have heard from pearl divers that the pressure increases the deeper you go, and she must have seen how cotton buyers can buy more cotton by compressing it, while those who are purchasing oil cannot. By combining these two sharp observations she found an apt analogy with which to make her point. Even plunged into the depths of the sea, a measuring cup brings up one cup of water, not four. Even a woman with wealth and a husband that suits her can only enjoy them to the degree allowed her by her past deeds, not more. Thus does Avvaiyar show the force of karma. In the West, knowing that pressure increases with depth, engineers have built dams to irrigate farmland and to store and make use of the force of water. Knowing that pressure does not change the volume of liquids, they have built hydraulic pumps and other useful devices. Avvaiyar, too, knew of such ideas and gave them to the world in her songs. The world rightly celebrates what she knows.

And now Thomas Hitoshi Pruiksma is giving to the West the Avvaiyar that was given to Tamil Nadu and to India. This is not simply a fact. It is a piece of great fortune. I have no doubt that the world will also celebrate this gifted young writer. May he be blessed with the friendship of wise men and women; may he become a writer of the highest kind. I give thanks to god who has brought us together—despite the differences between our countries—he as my student, and I as his teacher.

If on our old earth
There walk one upright man, for his sake
Everyone receives rain.

Dr. K. V. Ramakoti
Madurai, Tamil Nadu, India, 25 June 2007

LOVE GENEROSITY:

TRANSLATOR'S NOTE ON AVVAIYAR

Children in Tamil Nadu grow up with Avvaiyar. You can often hear grade-school students repeating after their teachers the opening statements of *Ātticcūṭi*, her alphabetical acrostic, one line for each Tamil letter, like "A is for Apple, B is for Ball." Her list begins: "Love generosity." Among her adages are "Forsake no quality," "Prepare no war," "Amend the earth and eat." Nine centuries later, many of her sayings still make sense, perhaps more so now than ever before.

As students grow older, they move through the longer lines of *Koṉṟaivēntan* to the quatrains found in *Mūturai* and *Nalvaḻi*. These short poems are so vivid and sharp that years after they learn them, men and women can still recite them by heart. I was once in Goa, hundreds of miles from Tamil Nadu, exploring the streets of an old town, when a friend and I overheard a group of Tamil-speaking men buying cashews in a small roadside shop. My friend, whose mother is Tamil, turned to the group and said,

"Here, listen to a poem that my friend knows." At his urging, I recited Avvaiyar's "Good done to a man of character." The men's faces lit up and one by one they approached me and shook my hand.

In a sense, I grew up with Avvaiyar too. When I was first learning Tamil in Madurai, Tamil Nadu, fresh out of college, I knew almost nothing about poetry. I hadn't intended to study literature at all; my sole aim was to speak and understand Tamil as it was spoken. My teacher, however, Dr. K. V. Ramakoti, started me reading *Mūturai*, insisting that I learn it by heart. Since I didn't yet understand the older language of the poems, all I could do was recite and listen to their sounds. By reciting and listening, though, I finally learned to listen, to hear the music that a line of poetry can make. Avvaiyar's poems are among the first that I came to love, in Tamil or any other language. I'm grateful for this chance to share them with others.

What follows are sixty of my translations of Avvaiyar's quatrains. The first set comes from *Mūturai*, "The Word that Endures," the second from *Nalvali*, "The Right Road." Both of these books are works on ethics, containing thirty-one and forty-one poems, respectively. The poems in the third set were composed separately and gathered into a collection by a later unknown editor. All sixty presented here exemplify a Tamil verse form called *venpā*, dating back to the late Sangam period. The particular kind of *venpā* that Avvaiyar used has a total of four lines: three lines of four feet (*cīr*) followed by a fourth line of two and a half feet. There is often a break between the third and fourth feet of the second line, giving the form what I find to be a satisfying dissymmetry. Although I don't think it's possible, or even desirable, to maintain the exact pattern of feet in English—a *cīr*, after all, is not quite the same thing as a foot—I have still tried to mimic something of the original form through lineation and through the relative length of lines.

In selecting poems to translate, I have been guided, on the one hand, by both my own sense and my teacher's sense of their qualities in Tamil, and on the other, by my sense of their translatability into English. Some poems, such as the last poem in *Nalvaḻi*, to which Dr. Ramakoti refers in his introduction, simply require too much explaining to make a satisfying poem in English. But others, by their juxtaposition of image and idea, offer possibilities to be carried into another language. Or so it has seemed to me. I have also included poems that are well-known in Tamil Nadu, as well as poems that, though dated and perhaps foreign to our sensibilities, nonetheless contain lines that sing.

A translator, of course, is never allowed to be satisfied. He can never share all that he wants to give away. But I've loved the generosity of Avvaiyar's songs. They have been for me a source of instruction and delight, and I hope these translations suggest at least some of that pleasure.

Thomas Hitoshi Pruiksma
Vashon Island, Washington, 1 September 2007

THE WORD THAT ENDURES

Poems from *Mūturai*

வாக்குண்டாம் நல்ல மனமுண்டாம் மாமலராள்
நோக்குண்டாம் மேனி நுடங்காது—பூக்கொண்டு
துப்பார் திருமேனித் தும்பிக்கை யான்பாதம்
தப்பாமற் சார்வார் தமக்கு

1.

நன்றி ஒருவற்குச் செய்தக்கா லந்நன்றி
என்று தருங்கொ லெனவேண்டா—நின்று
தளரா வளர்தெங்கு தாளுண்ட நீரைத்
தலையாலே தான்தருத லால்

2.

நல்லா ரொருவர்க்குச் செய்த உபகாரம்
கல்மே லெழுத்துப்போற் காணுமே—அல்லாத
ஈரமிலா நெஞ்சத்தார்க் கீந்த உபகாரம்
நீர்மே லெழுத்திற்கு நேர்

An able tongue, a good mind, a look from Fortune
Atop her flower, a body that doesn't falter—

All these
To those who bring flowers to the Lord, falling daily
At his trunk and red feet.

1.
When doing good to a man, do not ask
If he'll do good.

Tall-standing coconut palms,
Tireless and growing, take water at their roots
And return it, sweet, from above.

2.
Good done to a man of character—
Letters etched in stone.

Good done
To a man who lacks ethics and love—
Letters traced upon water.

4.

அட்டாலும் பால்சுவையிற் குன்றா தளவளாய்
நட்டாலும் நண்பல்லார் நண்பல்லர்
கெட்டாலும் மேன்மக்கள் மேன்மக்க ளேசங்கு
சுட்டாலும் வெண்மை தரும்

5.

அடுத்து முயன்றாலு மாகுநா என்றி
எடுத்த கருமங்க ளாகா—தொடுத்த
உருவத்தால் நீண்ட உயர்மரங்க ளெல்லாம்
பருவத்தா லன்றிப் பழா

6.

உற்ற இடத்தில் உயிர்வழங்குந் தன்மையோர்
பற்றலரைக் கண்டாற் பணிவரோ—கற்றாண்
பிளந்திறுவ தல்லால் பெரும்பாரந் தாங்கின்
தளர்ந்து வளையுமோ தான்

4.

Even when boiled, milk will taste sweet. Even when
Befriended, the unfriendly
                              are not friends.
Even when ruined, the great will be great. A conch,
Even scorched, gleams white.

5.

Try as you might, if the time isn't right
Nothing you do will get done.
                                    Thick,
Tall, imposing in stature, out of season
Fruit trees stand barren.

6.

Does he who gives life before he gives honor
Bow when he sees his enemies?
                                    Beneath a heavy load
A stone pillar may break, but tell me,
Does it buckle? Does it bend?

7.

நீரளவே யாகுமாம் நீராம்பல் தான்கற்ற
நூலளவே யாகுமாம் நுண்ணறிவு—மேலைத்
தவத்தளவே யாகுமாந் தான்பெற்ற செல்வம்
குலத்தளவே யாகுங் குணம்

8.

நல்லாரைக் காண்பதுவும் நன்றே நலமிக்க
நல்லார்சொற் கேட்பதுவும் நன்றே—நல்லார்
குணங்க ளுரைப்பதுவும் நன்றே அவரோ
டிணங்கி யிருப்பதுவும் நன்று

9.

தீயாரைக் காண்பதுவுந் தீதே திருவற்ற
தீயார்சொற் கேட்பதுவுந் தீதே—தீயார்
குணங்க ளுரைப்பதுவுந் தீதே அவரோ
டிணங்கி யிருப்பதுவுந் தீது

7.

With the water, the lily rises; with books studied
Climbs subtlety of mind.
Deeds in the past fix the wealth of the present;
Lineage, the limits of character.

8.

To behold a good person is good. To hear
His words full of meaning is good.
                                        To speak
Of a good person's character is good. Good
To find a place in his company.

9.

To catch sight of an evil person is bad. To hear
His words without meaning is bad.
                                        To speak
Of an evil person's character is bad. Bad
To find a place in his company.

10.

நெல்லுக் கிறைத்தநீர் வாய்க்கால் வழியோடிப்
புல்லுக்கு மாங்கே பொசியுமாம்—தொல்லுலகில்
நல்லா ரொருவர் உளரே லவர்பொருட்
டெல்லார்க்கும் பெய்யு மழை

12.

மடல்பெரிது தாழை மகிழினிது கந்தம்
உடல்சிறிய ரென்றிருக்க வேண்டா—கடல்பெரிது
மண்ணீரு மாகா ததனருகே சிற்றூறல்
உண்ணீரு மாகி விடும்

13.

கவையாகிக் கொம்பாகிக் காட்டகத்தே நிற்கும்
அவையல்ல நல்ல மரங்கள்—சவைநடுவே
நீட்டோலை வாசியா நின்றான் குறிப்பறிய
மாட்டா தவன்நல் மரம்

10.

The water that runs from the well to the rice
Also waters the wayside grass.

                              If on our old earth
There walk one upright man, for his sake
Everyone receives rain.

12.

Magnolias have large petals; honeysuckles, a sweet fragrance.
Don't judge a man small by his body.

                                    The sea is vast
Yet cannot clean hands. Beside it, the little spring
Yields sweet water.

13.

Standing in the forest with boughs and branches—
These are not great trees.

                              He, in the hall,
Who can't catch the speaker's meaning—he
Is a great tree indeed.

14.
கான மயிலாடக் கண்டிருந்த வான்கோழி
தானு மதுவாகப் பாவித்துத்—தானுந்தன்
பொல்லாச் சிறகைவிரித் தாடினாற் போலுமே
கல்லாதான் கற்ற கவி

15.
வேங்கை வரிப்புலிநோய் தீர்த்த விடகாரி
ஆங்கதனுக் காகார மானாற்போல்—பாங்கறியாப்
புல்லறி வாளர்க்குச் செய்த உபகாரங்
கல்லின்மே லிட்ட கலம்

16.
அடக்க முடையா ரறிவிலரென் றெண்ணிக்
கடக்கக் கருதவும் வேண்டா—மடைத்தலையில்
ஓடுமீ னோட உறுமீன் வருமளவும்
வாடி யிருக்குமாங் கொக்கு

14.

The forest peacock dances, and a turkey, watching,
Thinking himself similar, spreads his ugly wings
And struts.
                    Like that, the poem learned
By a man without learning.

15.

A doctor who ends a tiger's disease
Becomes its next meal.
                              Good done
To a man who lacks gratitude and sense
Is a pitcher cast upon rocks.

16.

Don't think to conquer the one who holds back,
Concluding he must lack sense.
                                        Perched on the sluicegate
Letting the running fish run, the white crane
Waits for the catch.

17.

அற்ற குளத்தின் அறுநீர்ப் பறவைபோல்
உற்றுழித் தீர்வார் உறவல்லர்—அக்குளத்திற்
கொட்டியும் ஆம்பலும் நெய்தலும் போலவே
ஒட்டி யுறுவார் உறவு

18.

சீரியர் கெட்டாலும் சீரியரே சீரியர்மற்
றல்லாதார் கெட்டாலங் கென்னாகும்—சீரிய
பொன்னின் குடமுடைந்தாற் பொன்னாகு மென்னாகும்
மண்ணின் குடமுடைந்தக் கால்

19.

ஆழ அமுக்கி முகக்கினும் ஆழ்கடல்நீர்
நாழி முகவாது நால்நாழி—தோழி
நிதியுங் கணவனும் நேர்படினும் தந்தம்
விதியின் பயனே பயன்

17.

Like water birds that leave a dried-up lake,
Those who flee trouble are not friends.

                                Like the lilies

And lotuses staying in that lake,
Those who stick with you—friends.

18.

Even when ruined, the noble are noble.
When the ignoble fall, what's lost?

                                Even when broken

A gold pitcher is gold. When a clay pitcher falls,
What's lost?

19.

A cup that is plunged deep into the sea
Cannot yield four cups of water.

                                Even if

Both wealth and husband are yours, past deeds
Alone shape one's pleasure.

20.

உடன்பிறந்தார் சுற்றத்தார் என்றிருக்க வேண்டா
உடன்பிறந்தே கொல்லும் வியாதி—உடன்பிறவா
மாமலையி லுள்ள மருந்தே பிணிதீர்க்கும்
ஆமருந்து போல்வாரு முண்டு

22.

எழுதியவா றேகாண் இரங்குமட நெஞ்சே
கருதியவா றாமோ கருமம்—கருதிப்போய்க்
கற்பகத்தைச் சேர்ந்தோர்க்குக் காஞ்சிரங்கா யீந்ததேல்
முற்பவத்திற் செய்த வினை

23.

கற்பிளவோ டொப்பர் கயவர் கடுஞ்சினத்துப்
பொற்பிளவோ டொப்பாரும் போல்வாரே—விற்பிடித்து
நீர்கிழிய எய்த வடுப்போல மாறுமே
சீரொழுகு சான்றோர் சினம்

20.

Don't think those born of the same body are brothers.

Fatal illness springs from the body too.

Medicines that heal grow in hills far away.

There are people like that medicine, too.

22.

Sad, ignorant heart! Do you think things happen

As wished? See how our fates are written:

                                        If the tree

That grants wishes grants stones to a man wishing,

Those stones are the fruit of past lives.

23.

Base men angered split like cracked stone.

Decent men, like pieces of cracked gold.

                                        Bow still in hand

The cut shot through the water closes. Like that,

The anger of great men.

24.

நற்றா மரைக்கயத்தில் நல்லன்னஞ் சேர்ந்தாற்போற்
கற்றாரைக் கற்றாரே காமுறுவர்—கற்பிலா
மூர்க்கரை மூர்க்கர் முகப்பர் முதுகாட்டிற்
காக்கை உகக்கும் பிணம்

25.

நஞ்சுடைமை தானறிந்து நாகங் கரந்துறையும்
அஞ்சாப் புறங்கிடக்கும் நீர்ப்பாம்பு—நெஞ்சிற்
கரவுடையார் தம்மைக் கரப்பர் கரவார்
கரவிலா நெஞ்சத் தவர்

26.

மன்னனு மாசறக் கற்றோனுஞ் சீர்தூக்கின்
மன்னனிற் கற்றோன் சிறப்புடையன்—மன்னற்குத்
தன்தேச மல்லாற் சிறப்பில்லை கற்றோற்குச்
சென்றவிட மெல்லாஞ் சிறப்பு

24.

As swans alight on a lotus-flowered pond,
The learned delight in learned company.

                                    Idiots
Without learning love idiots. By the pyre,
Crows long for the corpse.

25.

Knowing its own venom, the cobra lives in hiding.
Watersnakes lie about without fear.

                                          Those who have malice
Make themselves scarce. Those who do not
Do not hide.

26.

Between the king and the careful poet, the poet
Has greater glory.

                        Apart from his kingdom
A king has nothing. Every place a poet goes—
Praise.

28.
சந்தன மென்குறடு தான்தேய்ந்த காலத்துங்
கந்தங் குறைபடா தாதலால்—தந்தந்
தனஞ்சிறிய ராயினுந் தார்வேந்தர் கேட்டால்
மனஞ்சிறிய ராவரோ மற்று

29.
மருவினிய சுற்றமும் வான்பொருளும் நல்ல
உருவும் உயர்குலமு மெல்லாம்—திருமடந்தை
ஆம்போ தவளோடு மாகும் அவள்பிரிந்து
போம்போ தவளொடு போம்

30.
சாந்தனையும் தீயனவே செய்திடினும் தாமவரை
ஆந்தனையும் காப்பர் அறிவுடையோர்—மாந்தர்
குறைக்குந் தனையுங் குளிர்நிழலைத் தந்து
மறைக்குமாங் கண்டீர் மரம்

28.

A piece of soft sandalwood, even worn down,
Will not lose its scent.

                    Should his wealth
Wear away, will a victory-flowered king
Become thereby small of heart?

29.

Sweet relations, heavenly wealth, a radiant
Figure, a good family—

                        when Fortune comes,
These four come with her. And when she goes,
They go.

30.

As long as they can, the wise help
Even those who do wrong.
Till the day they chop it down, a tree grants
People shade.

THE RIGHT ROAD

Poems from *Nalvaḻi*

பாலுந் தெளிதேனும் பாகும் பருப்புமிவை
நாலுங் கலந்துனக்கு நான்தருவேன்—கோலஞ்செய்
துங்கக் கரிமுகத்துத் தூரமணியே நீயெனக்குச்
சங்கத் தமிழ்மூன்றுந் தா

2.

சாதி யிரண்டொழிய வேறில்லை சாற்றுங்கால்
நீதி வழுவா நெறிமுறையின்—மேதினியில்
இட்டார் பெரியோர் இடாதார் இழிகுலத்தோர்
பட்டாங்கில் உள்ள படி

5.

வருந்தி அழைத்தாலும் வாராத வாரா
பொருந்துவன போமினென்றாற் போகா—இருந்தேங்கி
நெஞ்சம்புண் ணாக நெடுந்தூரந் தாம்நினைந்து
துஞ்சுவதே மாந்தர் தொழில்

Milk and clear honey and jaggery and gram—
These four I will mix you and give.

                                    Elephant-faced
Noble grace-giving great ruby, give me
Tripartite Sangam Tamil.

2.

There are only two classes, to give it speech.
On earth, on the path that doesn't swerve,
The great give.

                    The base don't.
Thus say the books that endure.

5.

Plead as you will, what won't come will not come;
What is fitting will not go by saying go.

                                    To lament
In long thought, and make a wound of one's heart,
And then die is the labor of men.

7.
எல்லாப் படியாலும் எண்ணினால் இவ்வுடம்பு
பொல்லாப் புழுமலிநோய்ப் புன்குரம்பை—நல்லார்
அறிந்திருப்பார் ஆதலினால் ஆங்கமல நீர்போற்
பிறிந்திருப்பார் பேசார் பிறர்க்கு

9.
ஆற்றுப் பெருக்கற் றடிசுடுமந் நாளுமவ்வாறு
ஊற்றுப் பெருக்கால் உலகூட்டும்—ஏற்றவர்க்கு
நல்ல குடிப்பிறந்தார் நல்கூர்ந்தார் ஆனாலும்
இல்லையென மாட்டார் இசைந்து

10.
ஆண்டாண்டு தோறும் அழுது புரண்டாலும்
மாண்டார் வருவரோ மாநிலத்தீர்—வேண்டா
நமக்கும் அதுவழியே நாம்போம் அளவும்
எமக்கென்னென் றிட்டுண் டிரும்

7.

Looked at in all ways, this body is a hovel
For foul worms and teeming disease.

                              The great,
Because they know this, stand apart from it, silent,
Like water on a lotus's leaves.

9.

A river without water, in days that burn feet,
Will yet well from below and give.

                              Even in poverty
Those born to great families, when asked,
Will not say no.

10.

Even if you wallow, weeping year after year,
Will those who have died come back?

                              You of this earth
Weep not. That too is our way. Till going, give
—what is it to us?—give, eat, and live.

11.

ஒருநாள் உணவை ஒழியென்றால் ஒழியாய்
இருநாளுக் கேலென்றால் ஏலாய்—ஒருநாளும்
என்னோ வறியாய் இடும்பைகூர் என்வயிறே
உன்னோடு வாழ்தல் அரிது

12.

ஆற்றங் கரையின் மரமும் அரசறிய
வீற்றிருந்த வாழ்வும் விழுமன்றே—ஏற்றம்
உழுதுண்டு வாழ்வதற் கொப்பில்லை கண்டீர்
பழுதுண்டு வேறோர் பணிக்கு

13.

ஆவாரை யாரே அழிப்பர் அதுவன்றிச்
சாவாரை யாரே தவிர்ப்பவர்—ஓவாமல்
ஐயம் புகுவாரை யாரே விலக்குவார்
மெய்யம் புவியதன் மேல்

48

11.

If I say *give up food for one day*, you won't.

If I say *for two take*, you won't take.

O belly, full of pains,

You don't know one day of my grief.

How great, how rare, to live with you!

12.

The riverside tree and the regal life of kings,

Will these not totter and fall?

To plow and then eat

Is majesty without peer. All other work

Has flaws.

13.

Who can end those with life?

Who can keep men from death?

Who, in truth,

Can stop men from begging, here

On this beautiful earth?

14.
பிச்சைக்கு மூத்தகுடி வாழ்க்கை பேசுங்கால்
இச்சைபல சொல்லி இடித்துண்கை—சிச்சீ
வயிறு வளர்க்கைக்கு மானம் அழியாது
உயிர்விடுகை சால உறும்

16.
தண்ணீர் நிலநலத்தால் தக்கோர் குணங்கொடையால்
கண்ணீர்மை மாறாக் கருணையால்—பெண்ணீர்மை
கற்பழியா ஆற்றால் கடல்சூழ்ந்த வையகத்துள்
அற்புதமாம் என்றே அறி

17.
செய்தீ வினையிருக்கத் தெய்வத்தை நொந்தக்கால்
எய்த வருமோ இருநிதியம்—வையத்து
அறும்பாவம் என்னவறிந்து அன்றிடார்க் கின்று
வெறும்பானை பொங்குமோ மேல்

14.

Far worse than begging to make ends meet
Is to flatter, and jostle, and eat.

                          Awful.

Better to keep honor and give up one's life
Than fatten one's belly and live.

16.

Water from good land, greatness from giving,
Womanhood from faith,

                          clear sight from compassion.

On earth surrounded by seas, the wonder of those
Comes from these.

17.

Having done wrong, will great wealth become his
By shaking his fist at god—

                        he who had known

Our sins end on earth and when asked to give said no?
Will an empty vessel overflow?

18.

பெற்றார் பிறந்தார் பெருநாட்டார் பேருலகில்
உற்றார் உகந்தார் எனவேண்டார்—மற்றோர்
இரணங் கொடுத்தால் இடுவர் இடாரே
சரணங் கொடுத்தாலுந் தாம்

19.

சேவித்துஞ் சென்றிரந்துந் தெண்ணீர்க் கடல்கடந்தும்
பாவித்தும் பாராண்டும் பாட்டிசைத்தும்—போவிப்பம்
பாழின் உடம்பை வயிற்றின் கொடுமையால்
நாழி அரிசிக்கே நாம்

20.

அம்மி துணையாக ஆறிழிந்த வாறொக்குங்
கொம்மை முலைபகர்வார்க் கொண்டாட்டம்—இம்மை
மறுமைக்கும் நன்றன்று மாநிதியம் போக்கி
வெறுமைக்கு வித்தாய் விடும்

18.

Parents, children, family, friends, great countrymen
On this wide earth—

                              he who hates them,
Loving only things, gives only when he is battered,
Not when he is sheltered.

19.

By serving, begging, crossing bright seas,
Flattering, ruling, and singing—

                                        in hunger
And in vain we drive the body forward
For nothing but a cupful of rice.

20.

Like crossing a river with millstone in hand
The pleasure of a woman selling breasts.

                                        For this life
And the next, not good. It leads to poverty
And nothingness.

21.

நீரு நிழலு நிலம்பொதியும் நெற்கட்டும்
பேரும் புகழும் பெருவாழ்வும்—ஊரும்
வருந்திருவும் வாழ்நாளும் வஞ்சமில்லார்க் கென்றுந்
தருஞ்சிவந்த தாமரையாள் தான்

22.

பாடுபட்டுத் தேடிப் பணத்தைப் புதைத்துவைத்துக்
கேடுகெட்ட மானிடரே கேளுங்கள்—கூடுவிட்டிங்
காவிதான் போயினபின்பு யாரே யனுபவிப்பார்
பாவிகாள் அந்தப் பணம்

23.

வேதாளஞ் சேருமே வெள்ளெருக்குப் பூக்குமே
பாதாள மூலி படருமே—மூதேவி
சென்றிருந்து வாழ்வளே சேடன் குடிபுகுமே
மன்றோரஞ் சொன்னார் மனை

21.

Water, and shade, and land filled with grain,
And name, and renown, and good living.

                                  And home,

And wealth, and days. To those without malice,
She of the red lotus gives these.

22.

Listen, you wretched who toil and save
And bury your wealth beneath earth—

                                 When spirit

Leaves body, O worthless sinners, who
Will enjoy that wealth?

23.

Demons will come, white madars will flower,
Vines will creep up the walls.

                           Serpents will nest

And Misfortune move in to the house
Holding back in court.

25.

ஆன முதலில் அதிகஞ் செலவானான்
மானம் அழிந்து மதிகெட்டுப்—போனதிசை
எல்லார்க்கும் கள்ளனாய் ஏழ்பிறப்புந் தீயனாய்
நல்லார்க்கும் பொல்லனாம் நாடு

28.

உண்பது நாழி உடுப்பது நான்குமுழம்
எண்பது கோடிநினைந்து எண்ணுவன—கண்புதைந்த
மாந்தர் குடிவாழ்க்கை மண்ணின் கலம்போலச்
சாந்துணையுஞ் சஞ்சலமே தான்

29.

மரம்பழுத்தால் வெளவாலை வாவென்று கூவி
இரந்தழைப்பார் யாவருமங் கில்லை—சுரந்தமுதம்
கற்றா தரல்போற் கரவாது அளிப்பரேல்
உற்றார் உலகத் தவர்

25.

He who spends beyond what he has
Ruins his honor and knowledge—

                             a thief
To all, a seven-birth sinner, a scoundrel
To wife and mother.

28.

To eat, a cup of rice. To wear, a length of cloth.
And yet a person thinks a thousand thousand things.
Like an earthenware pot, the house without sense
Frets and worries till the end.

29.

When a fruit tree bears fruit, do people
Beg bats to come?

                    When a person gives freely,
As a cow gives milk, all the world's people
Become kin.

32.

ஆறிடும் மேடும் மடுவும்போல் ஆஞ்செல்வம்

மாறிடும் ஏறிடும் மாநிலத்தீர்—சோறிடுந்

தண்ணீரும் வாரும் தருமமே சார்பாக

உண்ணீர்மை வீறும் உயர்ந்து

33.

வெட்டனவை மெத்தனவை வெல்லாவாம் வேழத்தில்

பட்டுருவுங் கோல்பஞ்சில் பாயாது—நெட்டிருப்புப்

பாரைக்கு நெக்குவிடாப் பாறை பசுமரத்தின்

வேருக்கு நெக்கு விடும்

35.

பூவாதே காய்க்கும் மரமுமுள மக்களுளும்

ஏவாதே நின்றுணர்வார் தாமுளரே—தூவா

விரைத்தாலும் நன்றாகா வித்தெனவே பேதைக்கு

உரைத்தாலுந் தோன்றா துணர்வு

32.

Like drifts and hollows in rivers, wealth
Rises and falls.
                    Heirs of wide earth,
Serve rice, pour water. By giving,
The heart glows, and grows.

33.

Tough does not beat tender. Arrows
Pierce elephants, not cotton.
                              Rods of iron
Cannot crack stone, but a tree's green roots
Split rocks.

35.

Some trees, without flowering, bear fruit. Some people,
Without prodding, attain knowledge.
                                Even if you till,
Some seeds won't sprout. Even if you drill
Dolts learn nothing.

WHAT WE KNOW

Other Poems

வான்குருவி யின்கூடு வல்லரக்குத் தொல்கரையான்
தேன்சிலம்பி யாவர்க்குஞ் செய்யரிதால்—யாம்பெரிதும்
வல்லோமே என்று வலிமைசொல வேண்டாகாண்
எல்லார்க்கும் ஒவ்வொன்று எளிது

சித்திரமும் கைப்பழக்கம் செந்தமிழும் நாப்பழக்கம்
வைத்ததொரு கல்வி மனப்பழக்கம்—நித்தம்
நடையும் நடைப்பழக்கம் நட்பும் தயையும்
கொடையும் பிறவிக் குணம்

ஏசி இடலின் இடாமையே நன்று எதிரில்
பேசு மனையாளில் பேய்நன்று—நேசமிலா
வங்கணத்தில் நன்று வலியபகை வாழ்வில்லாச்
சங்கடத்தில் சாதலே நன்று

Can anyone make a bird's nest, a beehive, a spider's web,
A hill for the ants that chew wood?

                              Don't speak of strengths
With strong words, my friends. For everyone,
Something comes easy.

Practiced hands, good paintings. Practiced tongues, pure Tamil.
Practiced minds, knowledge that lasts.

                              By practice, a man
Walks miles. But a heart that melts, loves, and gives—
This comes from lineage alone.

Better not to give than give harshly. Better
To marry demons than a harsh wife.

                              Better to have
Enemies than friendship without love, and better
To die than live in want.

கற்றதுகைம் மண்ணளவு கல்லாத துலகளவென்று
கற்ற கலைமடந்தை ஓதுகிறாள்—மெத்த
வெறும்பந் தயம்கூற வேண்டா புலவீர்
எறும்பும்தன் கையாலெண் சாண்

மாடில்லான் வாழ்வும் மதியில்லான் வாணிபம்நல்
நாடில்லான் செங்கோல் நடாத்துவதும்—கூடும்
குருவில்லா வித்தை குணமில்லாப் பெண்டு
விருந்தில்லான் வீடும் விழல்

நேசனைக்கா ணாயிடத்தில் நெஞ்சார வேதுதித்தில்
ஆசானை எவ்விடத்தும் அப்படியே—வாச
மனையாளைப் பஞ்சணையில் மைந்தர்தமை நெஞ்சில்
வினையாளை வேலைமுடி வில்

What we know: a handful of dirt. What we don't:
The width of the world. The goddess of learning
Keeps learning.
                    So, poets, don't bet and talk big.
The body of an ant, too, is eight spans.

Life without means, business without brains, good government
Without a good country—not without possibility.
                                        But study
Without a guru, a wife without goodness, a house
Without guests—waste, waste, waste.

Praise a friend beyond measure in his absence.
Praise a teacher everywhere you go.
                                Praise your wife
On your pillow, and your children in your heart,
And workers when the work is done.

ஆலைப் பலாவாக்க லாமோ அருஞ்சுணங்கன்
வாலை நிமிர்க்க வசமாமோ—நீலநிறக்
காக்கைதனைப் பேசுவிக்க லாமோ கருணையிலா
மூர்க்கனைச்சீ ராக்கலா மோ

ஈதலறம் தீவினைவிட்டு ஈட்டல்பொருள் எஞ்ஞான்றும்
காத லிருவர் கருத்தொருமித்து—ஆதரவு
பட்டதே இன்பம் பானைநினைந் திம்மூன்றும்
விட்டதே பேரின்ப வீடு

தாயோடு அறுசுவைபோம் தந்தையொடு கல்விபோம்
சேயோடு தான்பெற்ற செல்வம்போம்—ஆயவாழ்வு
உற்றா ருடன்போம் உடன்பிறப்பால் தோள்வலிபோம்
பொன்தாலி யோடெவையும் போம்

Can a jackfruit be made a banyan? A dog's tail,
Made straight? A crow with black feathers,
Made to speak?
                    Can the dolt without love
Be made great?

Giving is virtue, earning rightly is wealth, living
In harmony and hospitality is love.
Letting go of all three, thinking only of god—
The bliss without peer of release.

With mothers go good meals, with fathers, good learning,
With children, the wealth one earns.
                                    With relatives,
Good living, with brothers, strength in arms,
With wives, everything, all.

NOTES

THE WORD THAT ENDURES

Invocation. By the time Avvaiyar wrote *Mūturai*, it had long been customary to begin books with a prayer song. Here she sings of the elephant-headed god Piḷḷaiyār, better known in the West as Ganesh. The color of his body is symbolic of greatness and traditionally associated with Lord Shiva, his father. "Fortune": Lakshmi, the goddess of wealth.

12. The flowers in the original poem are *tāḻai* and *makiḻ*, fragrant screwpine (*pandanus odoratissimus*) and pointed-leaved ape-flower (*mimusaps elangi*), respectively.

22. "the tree / That grants wishes": *kaṟpakam*, located in the realm of the gods.

THE RIGHT ROAD

Invocation. "Tripartite Sangam Tamil": both the Tamil of the three sangams or literary communities in ancient Tamil Nadu and the three kinds of Tamil literature: *iyal* (poetry), *icai* (music), and *nāṭakam* (drama).

2. "classes": in the original, the word *jāti* means both "kind" and "caste."

20. "a woman selling breasts": prostitute.

21. "She of the red lotus": Lakshmi.

23. "Misfortune": Mūtēvi, the elder sister of Lakshmi. "white madars": one of the names for *veḷḷelukku*. Other names in English include crown flower and giant milkweed.

WHAT WE KNOW

What we know. "The goddess of learning": Sarasvati. "eight spans": the human body measures eight spans (a span being the distance between the tip of the thumb and the pinky when outstretched).

Giving is virtue. "release": liberation from the cycle of rebirth

Acknowledgements

Poems 2, 10, 12, 20, and 26 from *Mūturai* first appeared in *Kavya Bharati* 17 (2005).

Poems 7, 8, 9, 17, and 18 from *Mūturai* first appeared in *Kavya Bharati* 19 (2007).

A version of "Love Generosity," poems 2 and 16 from *Mūturai*, 10 and 33 from *Nalvaḻi*, and "What we know: a handful of dirt" appeared under the title "What we Know: Poems of Avvaiyar" in the *Temenos Academy Review* 10 (2007).

A version of "Love Generosity," poems 1, 2, 6, 7, 10, 16, 20, 25, 26, and 30 from *Mūturai*, 7, 10, 12, 14, 28, 32, and 33 from *Nalvaḻi*, and "Practiced hands, good paintings," "What we know: a handful of dirt," and "With mothers go good meals" appeared in *Samyukta* (2007).

Printed in the USA
CPSIA information can be obtained
at www.ICGtesting.com
JSHW080006150824
68134JS00021B/2323